TRIAL ADVOCACY AND C

E

Joel Rook

TABLE OF CONTENTS

Published in 2018.

Thanks to my brother for editing and contributions.

INTRODUCTION

Take this with a grain of salt. Evaluate it for yourself and see if it is useful to you or not. If it's useful, great. If not, forget it. It amazes me that teachers seem to present their way as the one and only way and they fail to tell their students it's merely a suggestion for you to try out for yourself and see if it works.

Doing a trial is simpler than it seems, at least to me. In law school they gave us a textbook for our trial advocacy class: How to Win Trial Manual by Ralph Fine. It proposed a very simple approach to doing jury trials, and I have used the approach I formed based on it for the past 12 years.

The comment I usually get from judges or other attorneys is, "Your trials go fast!" And they do go fast because I focus in on the main points and don't throw any static out there. I tell the jurors the main points during the opening statement, I use the witnesses to support my main points, and I repeat the main points in the closing statement. Pick the main points and hammer them at least three times each. Make it simple and easy for the jurors. If you're lucky enough, you'll get some facts you can use to win.

I've won roughly 70 percent of my jury trials. If I get an acquittal on an attempted murder charge that carries a potential 25-year sentence, but the jurors convict the defendant on a count two that caries only five years, I count that as a win. Most of my clients are court-appointed. That means they can't afford an attorney and the judge appoints me to represent them. As a defender you're getting a case that has been vetted by both the police and the prosecutor, and they have determined that the case is strong enough to file a criminal charge. Most of the cases settle; of those that go to trial, I win 70%.

YOU AND CLIENTS

A lot of my trial wins come from "he said vs. he said" situations, where the decision turns on the credibility of witnesses. In contrast if I get police seizing drugs out of someone's pocket, that's tougher to win. You'd need a loophole to win that type of case – something like the state's drug testing lab lost the methamphetamine, but that doesn't happen often. A lot of times you get clients who are in deep trouble, for example a guy gets caught with 100 grams of methamphetamine in his pockets. Then he's hoping that you, his attorney, will pull a rabbit out of a hat and help him avoid a ten-year prison sentence, by finding some kind of loophole, for example, the evidence should be suppressed because the police searched him illegally. Defendants who are caught between a rock and a hard place -

looking at long term prison or a plea offer for a slightly lesser prison term – routinely assert all kinds of far-flung legal theories of how the police acted illegally during the investigation. Clients make these "Hail Mary" ridiculous claims because there is no other hope of winning. They want you to "fight for them" and do any kind of crazy thing you can concoct in order to throw a hammer in the works. File numerous intricate motions containing wild interpretations of caselaw, request continuances to delay the trial indefinitely, and they also resort to accusing you of being ineffective counsel. When a person is charged with a crime, there is so much pressure on them that it makes them lose their ability to see clearly. On top of that, a lot of the people charged with crimes are slightly out of touch with reality to begin with, and are also very persistent and aggressive in their assertions: their assertion that they understand the law better than you and that it should be interpreted in their favor, their assertion that the police mistreated them and did an illegal search and thus the evidence should be suppressed, their assertion that the case should be dismissed because the prosecutor and judge are biased against them, and that that they should win a civil lawsuit against the county in question.

Not all clients are like this. Some will make rational decisions with little or no complaining, but many won't. As I once put it during a legal education seminar I lectured at, there are some clients – difficult clients who the state has a strong case against - there is not a lot you can do to help them. You end up merely moving them through the legal process as they actively oppose each step. Part of the marketing side of the legal profession involves selling the public a fantasy that you are a super lawyer – better than the other lawyers – and that you can get them out of anything. That can give a desperate, terrified defendant a little bit of hope. Something you soon learn in practice is you should never kill a client's hope right away, especially in a harsh manner. You've got to do it slowly and gently, break it to them over time – perhaps allow them to come to the realization on their own, that there in fact will be a penalty – or else they will think you're not doing a good job as their lawyer. You're not "on their side and fighting for them". When I

visit my clients, often in jail or prison, I make it sound like I am

doing things for them, regardless of whether or not anything can

be done. And in fact, sometimes when it looks bleak at the

outset, a way to win pops up later on. So have an open mind. If I

can genuinely laugh about something with a client, I do, because

this helps them believe I'm on their side and not just "throwing

them to the wolves". Also, clearly explaining the case to the

client, in simple terms they understand, and leaving the choice

open to them on whether to plead or have a trial, helps instill

trust. Don't give the impression that they have to plead. Some

insist on "taking it all the way to the supreme court" no matter

what.

You can't let the inmates run the prison, you can't allow

the insane to run the asylum. Some loophole-seeking clients are

insistent on having things done their way, and if you want to stay

on the case you may choose to file many of their ridiculous

motions that lack real legal support, and have the judge deny

them, so the client feels like you've done something for them and are fighting for them, and it's not you denying the client's ridiculous loopholes, it's the judge. You pass the buck of responsibility onto the judge so you can still look like the good guy to your client.

There are some clients you won't want to represent. Sometimes you will tough it out and complete the case, sometimes you will get off the case. Early in my career I would put up with a lot of nonsense from clients, but these days I'm more likely to just get off the case. If I feel a genuine, searing hatred towards a client I will get off the case. Some of them I only dislike mildly, some of them I even laugh with – my favorites.

The first rule of law practice is C.Y.A.: Cover Your Ass. As a lawyer you find yourself in a hot-zone – a conflict zone wherein the client, especially hardened criminals, may see you as a target of opportunity in their quest to throw a wrench in the works, or get a second bite at the apple after a conviction by accusing you of screwing up their trial, accuse you of any manner of wrongdoing or professional shortcoming that can be concocted – in order to avoid serving their lengthy prison sentence. When you have a human being in a desperate situation they will do anything at all, with no regard for you or anyone else – to get out of it. Defendants also routinely ask if they can give the police information against others in order to get out of trouble. They turn on their friends, fellow drug users and dealers, their partners in crimes such as robbery and burglary. Once the authorities close in, such people are friends no more. It is a free-for-all in which everyone turns against each other.

My first year of practice I worked at a public defender's office and my boss told me to take off my tie and belt before entering the jail to visit clients. In most cases, inmates in county jail are not looking at a lot of time – they will be out soon. Aside from some mentally unstable ones, they are not likely to attack their lawyer. Lawyers have been attacked before but it has never happened to me, although I have had some clients whose hatred of me was not concealed at all. Some clients have a victim mentality and think everyone has wronged them and is conspiring against them, even though it is they who are preying upon the citizenry by means of forgery, robberies, burglaries, thefts, etc., and committing violent crimes. Their mentality is different that you are used to encountering in the normal world you inhabit of universities, shopping centers, corporate workplaces, recreational activities, home and family. These clients are not to be trusted, ever, in the slightest degree, no matter what, although you do have to investigate their claims and listen to their story, which often leads to useful information to use at trial. Every now and again you'll get a client who is violent and insane. The type that walks into the courtroom with a three-man security detail of the biggest deputies available, and upon entering the courtroom the client looks at the judge and says, "Fuck you," then he looks at you and says, "Fuck you too, worthless piece of shit." This type of client soon finds himself being wheeled into the courtroom, strapped into a special chair – a wheelchair but it looks more like an electric chair – with a muzzle on his face. Now and then an inmate with attack and kill deputies in the jail. This occurs in the prisons too. Sheriff's deputies tend to be easygoing and friendly in my experience – more than police or prison guards – and if they get too causal, an inmate can lunge, grab the gun off the deputy's hip, and kill the two deputies that were transporting him across the street to court. I was in court once when this happened outside the building during an inmate transport.

A comment I sometimes get from prosecutors is, "I like working with you – you're not one of the true believers." I tend to not get emotionally involved in my client's case – it's not that I try to stay even-minded, it just happens that way – a blessing perhaps. I just do my job and try to win trials because I kind of take pride in it and I get paid to, and I feel a duty to be diligent because this is important. Some would complain that unless you have a bulldog, all-in mentality, having your heart fully invested in your client's cause, you wouldn't do as good a job. In some sense, such a person, I believe, could do a better job by digging endlessly into every tiny detail, pursuing every single false lead, no matter how far-flung or ridiculous, to find a nugget of salvation for a client. For me in my practice, this does not result in any benefit to the client, other than thinking their lawyer is trying hard.

TRIAL STRATEGY

Voir dire is the process of selecting jurors to decide the outcome of a trial. My main strategy during jury selection is to tell my client, "If you get a good or bad vibe off of any juror, let me know." The "good vibe" people I keep, the "bad vibe" people I send home. Same goes for the vibe I personally pick up off the jurors. How I FEEL about them. The impression I get from them. It's that simple, and as I said, picking juries this way has resulted in a 70% win rate for me. In law school they tell you that if you're good you'll win 50%. The courts provide you with juror information sheets in advance that give some information about jurors, like profession, previous experience in cases, age, etc. But most of the sending home of jurors and keeping of jurors is based on the vibe – how my client and I feel when we look at the juror and how he or she answers questions during jury selection.

The prosecutor has a long list of questions they ask the jurors, so usually by the time I stand up to question them, I have only a few things to talk about. I mention the burden of proof, the presumption of innocence, and I may have a few hypothetical questions about things that are pertinent to the case – so I can get a feel for jurors' opinions and feelings toward the topic and towards my client, and also so I can plant a seed of why I should win the case. The jury selection is sometimes like the prelude to my opening statement. For example I might ask a juror what self-defense is if that's what the case is about. At least that gets them thinking about it, instead of just thinking my client is damned, which they will be thinking after listening to the prosecutor tell them what he's charged with.

Then we pick the jurors, we end up with 12 and a couple of alternates, and then we do the opening arguments. I proactively stick to my plan instead of weakening my argument by responding to the state's statements. In the opening statement I focus on my main points – what I have decided to make the case about – proactively and in favor of my client. I hammer these main points again and again throughout the trial. "I predict you'll hear that the alleged victim changed his story three times. The police will testify to this. You'll hear my client testify that the alleged victim attacked him. You'll hear that my client struck the alleged victim in self-defense. At the conclusion I'll ask you to find my client not guilty." Then the judge, with a pleased, perhaps bemused look on his face because I am not wasting time and because I clearly laid out the case, says, "State, call your first witness."

Before the trial I will have reviewed everything in the police reports and all other evidence I have, and I will have reviewed all of my notes, and decided what my plan of attack will be: my trial strategy, which I will execute at the trial. I will have interviewed my client in-depth and prepared him to testify, if that's part of my plan. He will know exactly what he will be testifying about and I will have him saying it in a way that doesn't sound rehearsed. I will also have listed out the exact questions I'm going to ask of the state's witnesses on cross-examination. That is because I do not want to be walking blind through a minefield and have those witnesses saying previously undiscovered, damaging things about my client. Also I do not want them repeating their story over and over so that it becomes more persuasive to the jury. I want to drop in and drop a bomb, get what I want out of them and get out. I want them saying exactly what I want and nothing more, and I want the jury hearing just that with no extra unnecessary words to dilute it. I will only ask a witness questions that I already know the answer to. I will only ask them, for the most part, questions that they are already on the record as having answered favorably to me – so that if they try to change their story I can pull out the record and make them admit they changed their story so the jury will see that they are fabricating their testimony. This happens more than you might expect. Before the trial we will have held a preliminary hearing where the key witnesses, or at least some of them, including the victim, will come into court and testify on the record, and a transcript is made of that, and I will have it in my hand at the trial in case I need, it. Also all the main witnesses will have given a statement to the police, and I can use the police reports to impeach them if they give a different story while testifying in court. Often it all comes down to a credibility contest – who do the jurors believe – the victim or the defendant. Part of the jurors' job is to evaluate the demeanor of witnesses as they testify in order to get a feel for who is telling the truth and who is not – and in my opinion, jurors are very good at doing this. Sometimes I don't know if my client is lying or not, and in those cases I may let them testify if I feel it will benefit us. Deciding whether or not to have a client testify often comes down to instinct for me. If a client's story is obviously bogus I won't allow it although it is their right to testify against my advice if they want. Some clients, stubbornly blind to the reality that people can see through ridiculous fabrications, insist on throwing multiple theories at the jury and seeing which one sticks – but that does not work. When you are seen as desperately throwing anything out there and hoping something sticks, providing multiple versions of the truth, providing ridiculous flimsy reasons why the police should not be believed – then you are not seen as the truth giver, and if the jurors do not believe you are telling the truth, you will lose. So you have to pick one story, a plausible one, and stick to it – at least that's how I do it. And I must reasonably believe the story is true or else I'm not presenting it at trial. In my job as advocate for my client, I take his or her story as if it is true, and I build a case strategy that incorporates it. If it is ridiculous I'm looking to get them to come off the idea of presenting that story to a jury.

Form time to time it looks like I'm doing so little during a trial that the client or their family will get mad at me and accuse me of incompetence, but then when I win, its all hugs and crying, and how great I am, and thank you. After the witnesses have testified the judge gives us a short break so the prosecutor and I can prepare our closing arguments – sometimes I go into the men's room and rehearse mine in the mirror. Then we come back and deliver them. The prosecutor goes first, then me, then the prosecutor gets to go again. Sometimes as you sit there and listen to the prosecutor's closing argument – you begin to feel like you are damned – your client looks really bad –it looks hopeless – but as the attorney you marshal your focus back to your plan of attack. Focus on the strategy you have created and will now execute – your main points from the opening plus anything else that came up during the trial. Then you get up and deliver it. If it's short you can say it all twice to make sure the jurors understand and remember it when they go into the jury room and discuss the case. There have been times I have done closing arguments when my client looks guilty, the state's evidence had been overwhelming, and the jurors are glaring at me. Early in my career I would not wear my eyeglasses during such a closing, so the jurors' negative reactions would not throw me off – but after experience it wouldn't throw me off regardless. Law school is enough of a gauntlet of training in professionalism, that no matter what you're feeling in court, you are still a professional and you do your job come hell or high water – you are doing a very important job that is an essential part of the bedrock of the law and order in this land. If people didn't get a fair trial in which they had an advocate tell their story, if we lived in an autocracy with a dictator who could do as they pleased – we would have a lower standard of living and we would live in constant fear. We live under laws, not just the law of the jungle. So regardless of whether your client is innocent or guilty, you have a job as part of the legal process to make sure that rules of that process are obeyed, to preserve peace and justice and prosperity for us all. I guess that's why I got into it in the first place – because I wanted to have a job of importance and I also wanted power, money, prestige, excitement, and I figured I might be good at it.

It is important to make a clear, simple, direct opening statement, so the jurors will know exactly what to look for during the witness' testimony, and so the jurors will know why you are asking witnesses the questions that you do, and what the testimony MEANS, why it is important, how it fits into the big picture that you laid out for the jurors in the opening statement. If you do not clearly, simply, and directly tell the jurors what the relevant points of the witnesses' testimony are and why it matters, then the jurors will not even notice the important points of the testimony as it occurs. This is why, in the opening statement, you clearly lay out for the jurors, simply and with no extra information that is distracting, what is important for them to focus on. Without this clear, simple, easy roadmap you have given them, they will not know what some of the testimony is relevant for. They will fail to focus on what you need them to focus on in order for you to win. A few inconsistencies in an alleged victim's testimony may seem irrelevant to the jurors unless you point out to them in an advance how very important it is. This is especially true since the state will try to minimize the importance of any such inconsistencies. If you wait until the end of the trial – the closing statement – to tell the jurors what to watch out for, to note the inconsistencies in a witness's testimony, then they may miss it entirely, or think it is of little consequence. That is why you win the trial right at the beginning by telling the jurors to focus on those inconsistencies, because it is often a credibility contest – who is more believable – the witness / victim, or your client the defendant, and you chip away at a witness' credibility by showing inconsistencies in their testimony – they have changed their story, and therefore what they say is not believable. This is why it is so important to focus the jurors, over and over throughout the trial, on your key points

– such as inconsistencies in a witness testimony – at least three times: at the beginning in the opening, then during cross examination of the witness or simply by questioning the officer about the witness' previous statement and then comparing it to other statements the witness has given, and then finally again in the closing argument. That way you repeat it to the jurors so they focus on it and are likely to consider it to be important, and not miss any little details relevant to it during the trial. By telling the jurors what your key points are at the beginning of the trial – during the opening – they are more likely to pay attention to that key issue and think it s relevant and watch out for details about it during the trial. You are directing their attention, shaping how they perceive the trial. You can even begin to insinuate your argument before the opening, subtly, during the jury selection, by asking general questions about the topic of your case. For example, when is it appropriate to defend yourself, juror? Must you wait until someone is already beating you to a pulp? Or, what is great bodily harm, juror? Is it an ankle sprain, or must there be more? These kinds of questions get the jurors focused on what YOU want the main issue of the trial to be: that this was self-defense, or that no great bodily harm occurred. And it probably can't be over-emphasized, you better deliver on the promises you make in the opening by backing up your main points with evidence, i.e. testimony and or other evidence. You shall not make promises during opening arguments that you cannot deliver on: that are not backed up reasonably by evidence. And, if your argument is ridiculous or obviously unbelievable or you are merely throwing out several alternative theories of the truth in a desperate attempt to confuse the jury or hope they will be bamboozled, you will lose. Some clients fail to understand that if their story is patently ridiculous, the jurors will see through it, but when you are looking at prison, any insanely false hope seems legitimate. If you burglarize someone's house and there is a believable eyewitness, and the victim's possessions are found at your house, the "it was some other dude" defense may not fly. Likewise any illusory hope and prayer of salvation by a ridiculous legal loophole seems plausible to many defendants. However in my experience the courts of appeals, who are the ones tasked with sorting out what the law is, seem to find ways to make the law mean whatever they want. And that means that anyone who is obviously guilty will serve the prescribed sentence. The court of appeals makes the law mean what they want it to mean, unless there is absolute legal authority which handcuffs them and makes them decide an issue one way or another. They will deny your appeal on six different minor procedural grounds. Most of the time there is no legal loophole to save a convicted defendant from going to prison. It is true that during the course of a litigation, many things can happen that are favorable to a defendant, but still overall, the odds of getting off on a technicality are small. The Court of Appeal only protects against egregious transgressions.

In your opening, don't make brash conclusions. Just make points that the evidence supports – all of your main points should be reasonably supported by evidence – and you should seem like you are letting the jurors make the conclusion themselves. Don't make any far-fetched claims based on flimsy evidence in the opening statement. If you do, jurors would see you not as the truth giver, but as an ignorant lawyer trying to mislead them. If you over-argue in the opening, the jurors would smell that you are not the truth giver, that you are trying too hard to make something out of nothing, that your client is guilty and you are trying to cover it up and present a false picture of reality to them. I like to take a professional / matter of fact / level-headed approach to drafting and delivery of my opening. However it's not necessary to deliver in a calm manner. During closing arguments when I am hammering points home again, I sometimes find that my delivery has some more emotion behind it. Part of that is because I raise my voice to emphasize points for the jurors, to be sure they pay attention. That may also be a natural part of the process since this is important – my client is looking at having years of their life – perhaps the rest of their life – dictated to them in prison, and after all this is the bedrock of American justice, so it is important, and whatever my shortcomings are as a man, and no matter how I feel, I'm going to do a damn good job, to the best of my ability. I want the jurors to see me as someone who is believable, reasonable, level-headed, not frivolous, not as someone whose perception is skewed because they have too much at stake, not someone whose emotions are clouding their ability to see clearly.

As the giver of truth, as a credible source whom the jurors can believe, it helps to acknowledge the state's damning evidence against your client – but don't focus on it, merely remove the sting of it. Show the jurors that you are aware of it and that you have considered it and that you're not trying to make them forget about it (actually you are hoping the jurors minimize the importance of or forget about the state's points) but don't be seen as trying to hide that part of reality from the jurors. You want to be seen as someone who has nothing to hide, who is not trying to hide any aspect of the facts from the jurors, who is not trying to distort the picture that they see, because the truth is on your side and you are completely fine with all of the truth being examined. You are unafraid. In fact that is how I instruct my clients to testify, especially on cross-examination. I tell them to answer the prosecutor's questions, directly and to the point, with minimal explaining or arguing, like you have nothing to fear. Do not try to avoid answering any question, even if you feel like it makes you look bad. Avoiding questions makes it look like you're scrambling to hide something. I want the jurors to see you answering without hesitation or fear, because the facts are on your side, you are telling the truth, and you have nothing to hide. It is best to simply answer the questions with a one-word answer if you can: yes, or no. If you need to say more, keep it to a couple of sentences. Don't ramble because it opens more doors of topics for the prosecutor to question you and make you look bad. Plus being direct and brief and not having to do a lot of explaining makes you look like you're telling the truth. If you have to correct the prosecutor, then do it. Yes, prosecutor, that is true, but I didn't hit the victim until he was charging at me with a knife. You can conclude your answer by bringing it back around to your story, your version of what happened.

In short, never be seen as hiding. Stridently and clearly present your case, proactively, as truth. Do not lose focus and get caught up in reacting to the state's arguments. You proactively execute your strategy at trial. Do not allow your focus to be jerked around by putting out fires. Stay proactive, stay focused on your trial strategy, focused on what is important.

Another benefit of keeping my trials simple is, the more things I have to focus on, the more likely it is that I'm going to forget something. The more complicated the trial strategy and the more issues there are to address, this also means more pressure on you as the lawyer, since you have to address it all. If you can simplify it for yourself and the jurors, it is better. You've been looking at the case for months, the jurors only get to consider it for a day or a few days, so keep it simple for them. Sometimes you get clients who insist on driving the bus – they want to control the trial strategy and give you orders on how to do it, and these clients inevitably want a bunch of red herrings – ridiculous and unnecessary arguments or considerations – put forth for the jury. Such clients would ruin their chances of winning if you were to allow them to drive the bus. They would drive it right off a cliff. When I have gone to trial with such clients, one way or another I have been able to do the case my way – the best way – instead of theirs.

TRIAL STRATEGY – CROSS EXAMS AND DIRECT

You USE witnesses to tell YOUR story to the jury. You elicit information from witnesses, including your client, for one purpose and one purpose only: to back up the main points, the story, the road map, that you laid out for the jurors at the beginning of the trial in the opening statement. You only ask questions that you already know the answers to and that will back you up. You argue your case to the jurors THROUGH the witness, like a puppet master. Sometimes unexpected things come out during testimony in trials, and yes you should capitalize on that, and ask the witness questions about it if you safely can, and incorporate it into your closing argument. However, blindly questioning a witness without knowing what they will say is like walking in a minefield and should be avoided at all costs, unless of course you deem it necessary. All rules may be broken and as a skilled advocate you'll develop a FEEL / intuition, as needed.

On direct examination, that is, having your client testify, you are not supposed to lead the witness. That means you are not supposed to put words in their mouth. For example, questions like, "You went to the house, right?" Are leading and generally forbidden, while, "Did you go to the house then or not," is not leading. You are supposed to let the client tell their story.

However, in fact you can use them to tell the jurors the story that YOU want told, and you should. Yes it is possible to win by just asking your client "What happened next?" over and over again, but this can result in rambling incoherent unfocused answers and in them forgetting to say the main points. Instead of asking them what happened next, you can offer them a choice in their answer, for example, "Did he attack you or not." Prosecutors can object to you as leading the witness, but by then the jurors already know what you're asking and what the answer is, and you can simply follow up with, "What happened next," and your client will know what to say. You are not putting the case in your client's hands to win for you, you are controlling what he says, according to your plan, in order to focus the jurors on the relevant points and win the case. You are in control of the entire process. Also, when you keep answers short and to the point like this as opposed to the rambling answers prompted by "What happened next," it becomes a back-and-forth interaction between you and the client, and this helps to hold the jurors attention better than a long rambling incoherent speech by the client. Notably, I have had clients who decide to say whatever they want when it's their turn to testify – including long, free-associated rants and the dropping of many F-bombs – and even then we won the trial.

Sometimes you'll get states' witnesses or victims who try to avoid answering your questions, or try to not answer them at all – even police will sometimes do this. "Officer, at one point the victim told you it was some other guy, right? Officer: rambling, off-topic answer. Me: Just to be sure officer, the victim DID at one point tell you that it was someone else that robbed the store, right? Avoiding questions makes the witness look bad in front of the jurors. I simply ask them again until they provide an answer, and I am professional about it and not rude.

As for objecting in front of the jury, I rarely do it, unless I feel it is something that would likely win the case on appeal for my client. This is because there is a risk that the jurors will see you as trying to hide the truth from them, or see you as being afraid of the truth coming out – but remember, you are not afraid of the truth, because it is on your side, and you are hoping that the jurors get to hear all of it – that is the way I like to appear during a jury trial.

LOOPHOLE LAWYERING

In trial litigation there are a lot of other things you need a basic understanding of – such as subpoenaing witnesses and evidence, knowledge of the rules of evidence, and how to do legal research. A lot of that is covered in law school. These things are all important and necessary but I don't classify them as being the main part of doing jury trials. Focusing on things like legal research, fine points of caselaw, and legal procedure, are almost a different sort of lawyering: loophole lawyering –

and it's a different niche than doing jury trials. Trials are more

of an overall feel, big picture endeavor. The loophole lawyering

– splitting hairs – having a mind like a trap and recalling every

little detail of the law – is a different and equally valid niche of

law. As a trial specialist I am more of a generalist than a

loophole lawyer. I know how to do loophole lawyering, and I am

able to do it to a degree, but there are those who are far better at

it than me. That is why, if I were ever to land a behemoth case,

I'd probably hire an assistant to be my loophole lawyer and

make sure we aren't missing any loopholes as we lumber

towards the trial. Part of the loophole game is in preserving

objections on the record: criminal, courtroom, legal, or

constitutional procedure where the judge, prosecutor, or police

have made a mistake – so that the court of appeals will reverse

the conviction and and the case will be dismissed or the client

will get a second try at winning. Part of the practice that I dislike

is that many clients are very intensely focused on loophole

lawyering and they expect you to do all kinds of fruitless things based on their hopelessly delusional understanding of the law. I do my best to accommodate clients' irrational requests, and when possible I dissuade clients from such notions – but often this type of client is of an insistent, overly stubborn type of mentality and will not be dissuaded. Some lawyers simply refuse to file their clients ridiculous motions and then the client asks the judge to remove the lawyer from the case, and the lawyer usually wants off the case as well. That is also an acceptable approach. Also, sometimes the judge does indeed make mistakes, for example, not saying the right words to the client on the record when having a client wave their right to a jury trial. Then the Court of appeals vacates the conviction and sends the case back to district court for retrial, and you can perhaps negotiate a better plea offer. So sometimes loopholes do work.

PROFESSIONALISM

Promises to pay me on the side, and occasional insinuations of sex. Any lawyer who makes even the slightest false step will later be accused by the client, who will be trying to avoid prison by doing so. Female lawyers who sleep with their male criminal clients will later be accused of unprofessional conduct by those worm-like male clients, in order to avoid their prison sentences. Nothing is sacred. If you are a male lawyer and you invite a female criminal client to stay at your house, you will one day come home to find that your house has been ransacked and the sheetrock busted out of the walls and all of the copper pipes stripped out because she invited her drug addict friends over and they took all your shit, plus all the copper in the house so they could sell it for scrap, and she will have disappeared into the wind.

In law school they tell you that the first three rules of the practice of law are: 1. Cover your butt. 2. Get the money up front. 3. No sex with clients. You have to cover your butt because the lawyer sometimes becomes a target at some point in the process. Therefore you have to do everything by the book and record it all, or else you could lose your license to practice law. As for the money, if you don't get it up front, you're not getting it at all. That's usually the case as far as I can tell. Some lawyers "work with people" on payments, but as far as I can tell, that's another way of saying the lawyer will accept less money than they are officially charging, because you never get all the payments. Third, if you as the lawyer have sex with the client, you have just handed the client the means of using you as a target, to get a second bite at the apple when they are dissatisfied with the outcome of their case, because the ethics commission in your state will see you as having a conflict of interest while representing your client and thus ineffective as counsel, and you will also be sanctioned or even disbarred as a result. A client will throw his or her lawyer under the bus when it suits him to do so.

TWO SIDES TO EVERY STORY

The fact remains that you must advocate for your client and investigate for him because often the prosecutor and police only uncover half the story and it is your job to bring the rest to light. It's human nature that we're only going to delve deep enough into the situation to do the job we've been assigned or to serve our own interests, and our perception is limited, and the police and prosecutor don't have an interest in your client being found innocent, their job is to convict people, protect the public from criminals. Ideally only guilty people would be found guilty, and prosecutors do have an eye on that, but the way it works

out, some of the story is always left untold, some of the evidence

not obtained or looked at closely – and it's your job to do that. If

you don't do it, people will be over-prosecuted. They will get too

much of a penalty for what they have done, in many instances.

Sometimes people who are innocent will be accused by

witnesses who seem to lie, with no awareness of their lies. Early

on it baffled me to discover that there are witnesses, victims,

people, whose memory of events is not based on facts, but on

their emotions, and they seem to have no awareness that this is

the case – so when they talk to the police they seem believable,

but upon closer examination, much of their testimony is a

complete fabrication. It is your job to bring out the truth, expose

lies and fabrications, and as an attorney you will feel a natural

responsibility to do so – at least I do and I think you will too. I

feel that the criminal justice system, including the police,

prosecutors, and the laws themselves – are at times overly

punitive, paranoid, and overly protective of the public, even in

those instances when the offender is a more or less normal

citizen who has made a once-in-a-lifetime mistake – and in those instances it is your job to advocate for your client, push back at the forces being brought to bear against him. In the overall picture we do need stern laws and we do need to look at offenders as a future risk, because many of them are what the law treats them as – some form of danger to society. It's not like a movie where all persons can be reformed. Some can't. I understand the statistics show that with proper treatment, some offenders, like drug offenders, and perhaps others like violent offenders, have a lesser chance of reoffending – about a 20% lesser chance if I recall – but that statistic may have changed over the past couple of years – and the specific percentage probably differs among types of offender. Sometimes repeated treatment works. People complain about drug offenders going to prison, but the alternative is to let them continue to use drugs, almost unabated by the effects of treatment – and either overdose, engage in reckless and destructive behavior while high, or commit crimes of all sorts to support their addiction. Perhaps we can come up with a more effective treatment.

Where I practice, cases involving methamphetamine users comprise over half of the criminal courts' dockets.

It used to surprise me that prosecutors themselves sometimes do things that are not allowed. Some will, perhaps out of ignorance, find an indirect way to ask a judge to break a plea agreement, "Well, judge, we DID agree to probation, but I would just ask you to consider the lengthy criminal history, the escalating violence, the drug use..." This is rare, and when it happens I act professional. I get plea agreements in writing and on the record and present my clients in the best light at sentencing. Some prosecutors will try to bring "experts" into court to testify at trial about the various evil things that certain types of defendants are capable of doing. This type of testimony is irrelevant and unduly prejudicial, under the rules of evidence – it has nothing to do with the facts at hand but is merely used to make the defendant look bad. For example there are "domestic violence" experts who will testify about the escalating cycle of violence and the ultimate horrible offenses that may occur when domestic violence situations escalate. They may present this testimony during a trial that involves none of those types of offenses but rather is about a minor domestic violence event. I will object to that, on the record, so the court of appeals will reverse any conviction that occurs.

From time to time a client will say something to me along the lines of, "When I get out of prison I'm gonna do this shit some more." Other career criminal clients will argue that they can turn their life around and be law abiding, or that they are being falsely accused. Some insist that they are being singled out for prosecution unfairly, that they have a job lined up and a sick relative to care for. As a politician you listen to all of this and don't call them out on it – at least that's how I do it- in order to preserve the working relationship you have with your client.

BUSINESS OF LAW

In doing what I do – specializing in criminal litigation – your advertising has to be good in order to earn a lot. I believe I'm good, maybe the best, at trials, and I offer a lot of value in other areas of the process. But when someone gets charged with a serious crime, there is often no way to predict with certainty what the outcome will be, no matter who your attorney is. So when someone calls me I'm not making promises or trying to make the prospective client feel good. I'm telling the truth, and I need the money up front – and most people don't have it sitting around – although you can propose creative ways for clients to obtain cash – like getting title loans on cars, getting cash advances on credit cards, payday loans, taking collections for family members, etc. As a lawyer you kind of do guesswork at every stage of the process. Can you do anything for the client? Should the client plead or go to trial? What's the cost of losing at trial? What's the chance of winning? How well can you predict what the judge would do at a sentencing? Most any judge will deny any loophole-type motion you file unless you have the legal authority soundly on your side, but sentencings are less predictable. It's good to know the judge's tendencies, but I have to admit that even after practicing with a judge for ten years, it can be hard to predict what they will do in close situations. Overall though, any judge is going to err on the side of protecting the public from even the slightest threat, and err on the side of putting offenders in prison, especially if that is the prosecutor's request. Judges see, time and again, defendants fail on probation, fail to beat drug habits, end up committing new property crimes to support their habits, and violent offenders reoffend. Notably there are some cases when just once in a lifetime, the causes and conditions came together to form a perfect storm of calamity in a normal guy's life and he gets in a fight with someone, and it's a one-off and will never happen again, but a lot of offenders, most in fact – are repeat customers.

Running your own law firm can be nice because you can do it how you want, but the burden is on you to get the clients, or you will go broke. And getting the clients is perhaps more important than anything else you do, short of retaining your license to practice law. Therefore studying marketing, including online marketing, i.e. writing effective copy and placing advertisements in the right places, may be a good investment. It can also help if you do other things like give yourself the appearance of authority by doing lectures, doing blogs, joining professional organizations, putting lots of relevant content on the webpage, becoming proficient in advertising, etc. As I see it, if you're going to start a law firm, advertising and getting clients is perhaps the most important thing of all.

MISCELLANEOUS

Some counties have jury pools that are more friendly to defendants, and there I have won a couple of trials that I felt I probably should have lost, so there is always some uncertainty in predicting the outcome of a trial. There have been trials where codefendants in a robbery have testified against the defendant, but the defendant was still acquitted – and this was amazing to me – but it happened. However generally a trial's outcome is significantly is predictable.

One issue you face as a criminal litigator is often you deal with bureaucracies. The people who work in bureaucracies are often assigned a narrow task and have no understanding of the bigger picture of what's going on in their organization – and at times those people proactively will not raise a finger other than to do the minimum required of them. I can't blame them, I suppose. Some of them are quite helpful, some of them are willfully doing the least amount possible, without any regard to how it effects you. The fact is that when dealing with bureaucracies, nothing gets done unless you, the lawyer, make it happen. At times it's like dragging a stubborn donkey through the mud. It is on you, and you alone, to make it happen. Getting evaluations for your client, setting up phone calls with clients in prison, getting things electronically filed in district court, getting access to sealed search warrants, getting court dates set, getting additional law enforcement witnesses interviewed and subpoenaed, getting the state to approve funding for a private investigator to take photos for your case.

There have been a few times I have gone into the maximum security wing of a prison to visit clients, and every time I am on edge because of the chance, however remote, that wonton violence may occur. As I see it, some of the guys in max have nothing to lose, so why not take out some frustration when they feel it. Once as my escort and I walked into the hundred-year-old maximum wing, I was struck by how much like a scene from a movie it was. Old hewn stone walls, very small cells all lined up two floors high against one wall, and my prison guard escort was a little blonde woman in her late twenties, pretty, about five foot three. What in the name of Jehovah are you doing here? The inmates were walking around because it was lunch, and a crowd came walking towards us as we walked through a wide corridor between two buildings. They were dressed in jeans and light-blue collared shirts, most of them were very buff, and the most striking thin was the absolute stone look on their faces, and the way they held their shoulders back, projecting power. I had never seen such stone faces. We passed through them and I was all nerves, knowing that if they had the desire to, my little escort and I could be killed. But nothing happened. Suffice it to say, wonton acts of violence happen in jail and prison, whether its an old inmate cutting a guard's throat when his parole is denied, or a gang of inmates severely beating a big insane violent inmate, or occasionally lawyers getting attacked, deputies or guards getting attacked due to some perceived slight, real or imagined. My understanding is that at least in the prisons, the guards allow some drugs to be brought in, to placate the inmates and minimize unrest.

What does it take for a defendant to be declared incompetent to stand trial? A lot. For a person to be declared so mentally incompetent that they do not understand the legal proceedings against them, or to be declared so incompetent that they are legally incapable of committing a crime, they must be flat-out completely crazy. I have had clients who are out of touch with reality, delusional, hallucinating, paranoid. The example of a client who thinks that aliens are beaming rays down onto his head and that a resulting light is coming out of his eyes and projecting newspaper clippings onto the wall, is not far from what can pass as competent to stand trial. Such a client can be medicated and perhaps "restored to competence", at least temporarily, but that won't last.

In some states, felony sentences are determined based on a sentencing grid that considers the severity level of the felony and the offender's criminal history. More history, higher sentence. More severe felony, higher sentence. There are also special rules that increase sentences for repeat offenders of various types, and for felonies committed with firearms, and for a number of other circumstances. Typically a convicted defendant will receive the sentence from the grid, or some lesser amount of prison time, or probation, if the parties have a plea agreement. Plea agreements benefit the prosecutor by relieving them of the need to take every case to jury trial, which can be time consuming. For the same reason agreements also benefit the court. The defendant typically benefits by receiving a lesser sentence than the grid prescribes, or by having a companion case dismissed, or by having counts dismissed, which results in a lesser sentence, or at times, by the state agreeing to not file additional cases they have waiting. Most cases are resolved by agreement, but some make it to trial because it is a very serious case and the plea offer is not much better than simply being convicted at trial and receiving the sentence from the grid. When an offender is a serious danger to the public, the prosecutor will make a point of putting that person in prison for as long as possible. In that case there will not be a plea offer. Robbers, burglars, those who attack others especially in a way whereby serious harm can result, those who flee from police in their cars, and drug dealers usually fall into this category. Or if a person is a multiple repeat offender of small offenses like forgery, theft, drug possession, the same applies. The plea process is very formal and all recorded to insure it is done properly. The judge reads the person their trial rights under the U.S. constitution and the person pleads guilty. In small cases the defendant is then placed on probation, and most probationers fail their probation. Usually the court is lenient when a probationer has a urine analysis show drug usage or when they or miss an appointment of get a new misdemeanor charge, but once someone picks up a new felony or absconds, completely stops going to their probation appointments, the person is in danger of serving their underlying prison sentence. In the overwhelming majority of probation cases, the offender is a drug addict, and continues using drugs. As a result I find myself in court telling the judge their excuses, which generally results in the person getting a second, third, or fourth chance on probation after a jail sanction, then finally the judge orders them to serve the original sentence or some lesser version of it.

CONCLUSION

In a suit and tie you feel more professional and people treat you with a little more deference and respect. They're also more likely to say hello. I also like to wear a hat. Hats haven't been in style where I practice so I've kind of been a trailblazer and started to bring hats back. I found a straw hat at Whole Foods grocery, it's a throwback, like a classy guy in the 1950's might wear – and people love it. Old people smile at me and tell me they love the hat. As a matter of fact, adults of all ages do the same. The courthouse guards at the metal detectors typically have some banter with me and it often revolves around the hat. Maybe the suit and the hat give people some sense of order and old-time values, like there are gentlemen in the world who treat others with kindness and civility and friendliness, and there is authority and clear boundaries that we can feel secure within. I have grown to enjoy wearing the suit and tie and over the years I have began to appreciate fine clothing – something I never predicted would occur. As time passes and your life unfolds, the days and years contain new discoveries. Sometimes in a silent moment I notice myself and wonder, who the hell is this guy? In the original manuscript I had a paragraph on meditation here but I deleted it. At continuing legal education seminars they tell us about relaxation techniques like meditation and coloring in coloring books – imagine a roomful of lawyers coloring in a sketch of Ruth Bader Ginsburg. Probably not for everybody. But for some it is a good practice. Anyway, keep in mind that much of the dicta about dealing with clients in this manuscript was culled from the times when things did not go smoothly, so it kind of paints a one-sided picture of client relations.

Made in the USA
Lexington, KY
06 May 2019